# The Unconventional Guide to Praying in the Courts of Heaven: A Step by Step Approach to Courts of Heaven Prayers

The author is aware that the application of this book may differ from one person to another as such things as faith, persistence, trust, and love for God can determine the outcomes that you receive from the application of the principles in this book.

# TABLE OF CONTENTS

# CHAPTER 1

## Understanding the Justice System of Earth

When the children of Israelite were in the wilderness, it became necessary for their lives to be administered through a system of justice. Since the Israelites were living among each other, if there was nothing to guide them, the whole situation would have been chaotic. Whenever a person is offended, he will resort to self-help to get justice from the offender. God knew that this would have presented a situation where the society of the Israelites would have been destroyed as a result of retaliation. So he reduced something into what is called a code of conduct for the children of Israel in the wilderness. It was this code that was handed to Moses as the Ten Commandments which was later reduced into several rules that the children of Israelite have to comply with.

Exodus 21:28-30

> *If an ox gore a man or a woman, that they die: then the ox shall be surely stoned, and his flesh shall not be eaten; but the owner of the ox shall be quit.*

> *29 But if the ox were wont to push with his horn in time past, and it hath been testified to his owner, and he hath not kept him in, but that he hath killed a man or a woman; the ox shall be stoned, and his owner also shall be put to death.*

> *30 If there be laid on him a sum of money, then he shall give for the ransom of his life whatsoever is laid upon him.*

For instance, if someone is gored to death by an ox belonging to another person and that particular animal has been known to have gored some people to death before, there is a particular penalty that the owner of the ox must pay. This is because the owner of the animal has known that he has a dangerous animal, and he ought to have prevented the animal from causing injury to other people. Several provisions in the Bible regulate the children of Israelite in the wilderness such as when someone steals the animal of another, or when that person engages in acts that cause a breach of peace in the wilderness. The justice system was provided for that person to restore what he has taken. It was the system of administration of justice that was running in the wilderness to ensure peaceful coexistence among the Israelites.

The conflict in that ancient society was so great to the extent that Moses was overburdened by the cases that were coming out from the people daily. It took the intervention of his father in law who gave him wise counsel on how to handle these several cases that were coming from the people. Moses had to appoint some people as magistrates to help him with the administration of justice.

As society grew and changed, justice was never left out. And any time that justice was left out, the operation of the society was upside down. And I will show you what happened in the Bible when justice was left out and the nature of the society at that time.

Judges 18:7

> *Then the five men departed, and came to Laish, and saw the people that were therein, how they dwelt careless, after the manner of the Zidonians, quiet and secure; and there was no*

> *magistrate in the land, that might put them to shame in any thing; and they were far from the Zidonians, and had no business with any man.*

As a result of the absence of magistrates in the land, the Bible says the people were living carelessly after the manner of the Zidonians. So a society where justice is not in place is one that everything will be out of order.

Although the administration of justice in modern times has changed from what was obtainable at the time of the children of Israelites when they were in the wilderness, it is a change in the method of application of justice than the justice itself. What I mean is that although the way of applying justice might have changed, justice is still been applied anyways. This foundational understanding is very important for praying in the courts of heaven because your knowledge of the justice system will help you to pray in the courts of heaven effectively.

It doesn't matter the type of country that you visit, they have their type of justice system that is administered either by judges or magistrates as the case may be. When someone does what is wrong he is brought to the courts for them to determine that conduct whether is deserving of punishment. This is necessary for society to be kept to prevent a situation where people take the laws into their hands to take vengeance against those who offended them. Even when the matter has been determined by a particular court, one of the parties who was dissatisfied by the way the court conducted the case might appeal, go to a higher court to see if he may get justice. It's this system of justice that has kept society together. Imagine a society where there is no judge, no law, and everyone does what he pleases. If someone committed a crime, he can't be arrested. If someone kills another person, he can't be touched. Imagine a society where law and order are not allowed to run its full cause. What will that kind of society portend for its members? Your answer is as good as mine, it will always be chaos and disorder. If that kind of society continues in that manner it will soon descend into war. Have you seen the importance of justice in society? In the same way that we have a justice system of the earth that is how there is a justice system that rules in heaven too. We'll come to that shortly but you need to have this proper understanding so that when you are coming into the courts of heaven to pray, you are doing the prayers not as a result of a custom or tradition, but from the basis of your deep understanding of scripture.

## Understanding the system of heaven

When the land of Sodom and Gomorrah committed atrocities before the eyes of the Lord, it became necessary for heaven to respond as a result of the justice of God. The reason why believers call God a faithful God is because he is just. The justice of God means that he will always do what is right in every circumstance. That is, God will always give you what you deserve that's justice. So the land of Sodom and Gomorrah was deserving of the justice system of heaven, and it became necessary for God to take any action concerning the evil ways of the land. However, there was someone in that land who was living a righteous life and God will be unjust to condemn both the wicked and just at the same time. Lots, cousin of Abraham was in that land which was due for the wrath of God. Since God will always give someone what he deserves as a righteous God, the land of Sodom and Gomorrah has been marked by heaven for destruction. The Bible tells us that righteousness and justice are the foundation of his throne. If righteousness and justice are the basis upon which the foundation of the throne of God is standing, then it would be contrary to the nature of God to show any form of injustice. Although what happened between Abraham and God concerning his intercession for the land of Sodom and Gomorrah because of his cousin, Lot may not be courts of heaven prayer, it was an appeal directly to the justice of God.

Genesis 18:23-33

*And Abraham drew near, and said, Wilt thou also destroy the righteous with the wicked?*

*24 Peradventure there be fifty righteous within the city: wilt thou also destroy and not spare the place for the fifty righteous that are therein?*

*25 That be far from thee to do after this manner, to slay the righteous with the wicked: and that the righteous should be as the wicked, that be far from thee: Shall not the Judge of all the earth do right?*

*26 And the Lord said, If I find in Sodom fifty righteous within the city, then I will spare all the place for their sakes.*

*27 And Abraham answered and said, Behold now, I have taken* upon me to speak unto the Lord, which am but dust and ashes:

28 Peradventure there shall lack five of the fifty righteous: wilt thou destroy all the city for lack of five? And he said, If I find there forty and five, I will not destroy it.

29 And he spake unto him yet again, and said, Peradventure there shall be forty found there. And he said, I will not do it for forty's sake.

30 And he said unto him, Oh let not the Lord be angry, and I will speak: Peradventure there shall thirty be found there. And he said, I will not do it, if I find thirty there.

31 And he said, Behold now, I have taken upon me to speak

*unto the Lord: Peradventure there shall be twenty found there. And he said, I will not destroy it for twenty's sake.*

*32 And he said, Oh let not the Lord be angry, and I will speak yet but this once: Peradventure ten shall be found there. And he said, I will not destroy it for ten's sake.*

*33 And the Lord went his way, as soon as he had left communing with Abraham: and Abraham returned unto his place.*

Abraham started his prayers by telling God that if you find fifty righteous men in the city of Sodom and Gomorrah, will you destroy it? Abraham continued to appeal to the justice of God until he ensured that the life of his cousin was spared from the destruction that was awaiting the land of Sodom and Gomorrah. It was Abraham's reliance on the justice of God that led to the rescue of his cousin Lot.

When Lucifer who was one of the Princes in heaven sinned against God, the justice system of heaven demands that action against Lucifer be taken. It was for this reason that Lucifer was cast out of heaven by Michael and the other host of angels. It is the same situation that happened in the Garden of Eden when God had commanded Adam and Eve not to eat of the fruit of the knowledge of good and evil. When they decided to violate the commandment that God gave them, again the justice system of heaven means that God has to respond in one way or the other. Another response was to have the man and the woman chased out of the Garden of Eden. God who is just will always respond in this manner because he is just. It was from the elaborate prayer of Abraham on that day when he was interceding for the land of Sodom and Gomorrah that he explained to us that God who is the judge of all the earth will always do what is right. And it was for this singular reason that lot was spared. If not, he would have been overtaken by the overthrow of the land of Sodom and Gomorrah.

Friends, I want you to have this proper understanding so that you can know how to pray in the courts of heaven and come out with an instant answer. Whenever a wrong has been committed against you, the justice administration of heaven implies that God has to respond to that wrong that has been done against you. What could that wrong be? It could be witchcraft oppression against your life. It could be an attack on your finances. It could even be an attack on your health. Or it could even be a man who has stood in the way to say that as long as he is a life, you will never have peace. By that wrong that has been committed against you, God will respond. It is my personal belief that the consuming fire of God has been reserved for some of the responses that come out from his justice as God.

The Bible tells us that in the book of Hebrews chapter 12 that God is the judge of all. He is the God that will judge both the living and the death. It is the same God that has judged all the Princes of darkness because the Bible tells us in the book of John that the prince of this earth has already been judged. That is what the justice of God entails that whenever a wrong has been done against the believer, he will respond. The beauty of praying in the courts of heaven to activate the justice of God is that everything that you would ever pray for, has been purchased by the precious blood of Jesus. As you are praying in the courts of heaven there is an intercession through the blood of Jesus that is going on for you. And by Scripture, we know that the blood of Jesus speaks better things than the blood of Abel. While you are praying in the courts of heaven the blood of Jesus will be making intercession for you that remember I died for this person and gave my life for him so that he can have these things.

# CHAPTER 2

## Court Participants

In every court system, some participants keep the court active. If you walk into a conventional court system, for instance, there are some common individuals that you will see. You will see the lawyers in the Courts, you will see the litigants who may be the defendant or the plaintiff. Then you will ultimately see the judge who administers justice to both the party at fault and who is not. Without these individuals in the conventional court system, it will never function well. It is the parties, the lawyers, and the judges that keep the court running.

In the same vein, whenever you approach the courts of heaven for a courtroom prayer are Courts of Heaven prayers, there are personalities that you will meet in that court.

## God the Father as a judge

We have already seen in the book of Hebrews, that God is the judge of all. He is the one who judges both the living and the death, he is the one that will judge both the unrighteous and the righteous. The entire administration of the Justice of heaven rests on him. When a man does anything deserving of the judgement of God, it is God the Father who issues that order that this person is judged. The event that ensured in the book of Acts chapter 5 when Ananias and Sapphira were judged for lying to the Holy Spirit, actually proceeded from the throne of grace, which God the Father administers. Although Ananias and Sapphira lied to the Holy Spirit and it is possible it was the Holy

Spirit that executed the judgement, but it was God who gave the order but the Holy Spirit executed it. The Bible tells us that the Holy Spirit will not say anything of his own, but whatever he hears, that is what he will say.

John 16:13

> *Howbeit when he, the Spirit of truth, is come, he will guide you into all truth: for he shall not speak of himself; but whatsoever he shall hear, that shall he speak: and he will shew you things to come.*

Everyone that has ever received the judgement of God came from the throne of grace, for which righteousness and justice are its foundation.

**The Holy Spirit, your intercessor**

In all prayers in the courts of heaven or in all type of prayers that the believer would offer in his lifetime, the only person who has been given the mandate to intercede on your behalf on the earth is the Holy Spirit. The petition you are presenting before the courts of heaven may be deeper than you can understand. While you are presenting your case before the courts of heaven on the surface, the Holy Spirit who has the duty of searching the depth of God, will search and help you to present your case adequately. This becomes necessary, especially where the believer has gone into the courts of heaven and begins to pray in other tongues. The Bible says in the book of Romans that we don't know how to pray as we should but the Holy Spirit will make intercession for us with groanings that cannot be uttered.

Romans 8:26-27

> *Likewise the Spirit also helpeth our infirmities: for we know not what we should pray for as we ought: but the Spirit itself maketh intercession for us*

*with groanings which cannot be uttered.*

*27 And he that searcheth the hearts knoweth what is the mind of the Spirit, because he maketh intercession for the saints according to the will of God.*

The Holy Spirit will be able to tell God that although your son isn't presenting this particular aspect of the petition before your throne as a result of his inability to understand certain things, I am making this intercession on his behalf through this present prayers in the courts of heaven that this other aspect of the petition that has not been brought before your courts be entertained, given an opportunity to be heard and granted. It is for this reason that every believer who wants to be a successful prayer warrior in the courts of heaven must understand the working of the Holy Spirit as he prays in the courtroom.

Friends, a believer must be sensitive to the leading of the Holy Spirit as he enters into the courts of heaven to offer his petitions. It is the Holy Spirit that can tell God the details of the petition you are presenting before the courts of heaven. Let me give you an example, you may be presenting a case of witchcraft oppression against your life in the courts of heaven, seeking that the justice of God is invoked for the destruction of witchcraft attacks against you. But you are not aware of the history of that attack that it had been running in your family. When you are presenting your case before the courts of heaven for the destruction of that witchcraft attack, the Holy Spirit will help you with intercession by telling God that the witchcraft attack has been going on from one generation to another, hence the generational root cause of this attack be destroyed so that your son or daughter can be free. Can you now see the importance of the third person of the Trinity, the Holy Spirit, in your prayers in the courts of heaven? Once you can work together with the Holy Spirit in your prayers in the courts of heaven, 100% success is always guaranteed because the Holy Spirit is the master in intercession. In this field, no spirit in the heavens or on the earth can rival his mastery.

Friends, any time you want to go into the Courts of Heaven to pray never forget to invite the personality of the Holy Spirit, with him, you can pray with ease. Sometimes the Holy Spirit can make intercession for you directly before the throne of grace for your case to be heard speedily and granted. In other times, the Holy Spirit may simply impress that particular area of your petition which you don't know in your heart so that you can pray it in the courts of heaven. In either way, the Holy Spirit is an indispensable helper when it comes to praying in the courts of heaven and any believer who wants to be successful in courts of heaven prayer must not ignore the ministry of the Holy Spirit in this area. After all, the Bible says we don't know how we are to pray but it is the Holy Spirit that helps our infirmities – inabilities, lack of understanding of the situation under reference, or sometimes as a result of the burden of what we are going through we are not able to present our case before God as we ought to. That is where the ministry of the Holy Spirit comes to the rescue of the believer in areas where your weaknesses are abundant, the intercessory ministry of the Holy Spirit is more than sufficient.

When Jesus was on the earth with his disciples, he was the one directly making intercession for them. When he was about to be arrested in the garden of Gethsemane there was something remarkable that he said to those who came to take him. Jesus said, if it is me that you are looking for, then let these go. And they let the disciples go. The Scripture is full of several instances that Jesus went to a quiet place to pray. And most of these prayers were for his disciples and his ministry on the earth. When Peter's faith was about to crumble, Jesus told Peter that I have prayed for you that your faith will not fail. So

Jesus was interceding for the disciples while he was on the earth. Now that he's gone into the heavens, who is it that makes intercession for God's children on the earth? It is the Holy Spirit. A prayer with the leading of the Holy Spirit is potent and powerful and it is the type of prayer that will readily produce results.

## Jesus as the advocate

While the Holy Spirit is the personality that intercedes for the believer on the earth when he is praying to God when it comes to interceding for us before the Father in heaven it is the exclusive job of Jesus Christ, our advocate.

1 John 2:1-2

> *My little children, these things write I unto you, that ye sin not. And if any man sin, we have an advocate with the Father, Jesus Christ the righteous:*

*2 And he is the propitiation for our sins: and not for ours only, but also for the sins of the whole world.*

You need to understand the important role that all these personalities play in your prayers in the Courts of Heaven. So that whenever you are entering the courts of heaven for prayer, there is an air of confidence that will hang around your faith. You have the Holy Spirit that intercedes for you right here on the earth. At the moment you enter into the courts of heaven, you have another intercessor that advocates for you before God in the courts of heaven which is Jesus Christ. Then, there's God the Father who sits on the throne of grace to administer that justice in the courts of heaven when you have presented your case. Isn't this beautiful? Praying in the Courts of Heaven is one of the ways to get your answers speedily because of the involvement of the three personalities of the Godhead – The Father, The Son, and The Holy Spirit. It will be impossible for you to have the three personalities of the godhead behind you and for your answers not to be granted. Except you fail to observe the protocols of coming into the courts of heaven to present your case. If you do the needful as a child of God before going into the Courts of Heaven, nothing will prevent you from coming out without an answer.

## The Believer as the Presenter of his Case

Two things happen when you come into the courts of heaven to present your petition before the Lord. There are parts of the petition which you present before the courts of heaven by yourself. And there are other parts of the petition that Jesus and the Holy Spirit will make on your behalf. The Holy Spirit will present the aspect of the case that is beyond your understanding while the one you know, as a human being, you present it by yourself. In all courts of heaven prayers, there is always a presenter of the petition. The person who presents his case before the throne of grace is the child of God, in this case, the believer who has come before the courts of heaven requesting for one form of justice or the other. It's the same thing that happens in the conventional court when an individual takes his case before a judge and tells the judge the entire story of the case so that the judge using the facts of what has been presented before him can do justice to both of them. That is how the courts of heaven work. Any believer who can have a proper understanding of the personalities of the godhead and the kind of different roles they play can state his case successfully and get an answer.

# CHAPTER 3

## What I need to know as a Beginner in the Courts of Heaven

## Access to the courts

The tearing of the temple curtains on that day when Jesus was crucified on the cross of cavalry means that every believer, big or small, a man of God or child of God all have access to God and by extension the Courts of Heaven.

Matthew 27:51

> *And, behold, the veil of the temple was rent in twain from*

*the top to the bottom; and the earth did quake, and the rocks rent;*

It is the blood of Jesus that gives us access to the holy of holies. Without the shedding of the blood, there can never be any form of access by any human being into the courts of heaven where God administers everything. And as a child of God, you have access into the Courts of Heaven through the blood of Jesus. I want you to be armed with this understanding that every time you go into the courts of heaven for courtroom prayer, always remember that the blood of Jesus is the only factor that has given you access into the courts. Before the tearing of the temple curtain, a lot of things including our sins stood as a barrier to having access to the courts of heaven. The moment Jesus died through the shedding of the blood on the cross of Calvary, access to the courts of heaven has been granted to all God's children. So the first thing that you need to know is that access has been granted to you by the blood of Jesus.

## Everyone can pray there

One of the myths concerning the Courts of Heaven prayer is that it is left for the super-spiritual. But that is not true. Everyone can pray in the courts of heaven and receive answers from God provided the person has a proper understanding of the procedures and protocols for gaining access into the courts. If someone is travelling to America, there are certain procedures that he needs to follow. That person must first apply for a visa to travel to the United States of America. On arrival to the United States of America, he must also present all his valid documents at the airport. It is after all these procedures have been adequately followed that the person can have access to the country. That is the same thing that happens when you want to enter the courts of heaven. You must follow the procedures laid down for you to have access to the courts. If you want to come and see the president of the United States of America or the president of a particular country, are you going to come there carelessly? I believe that if the president of America is extending an invitation for you to come into the White House, you might naturally wear your best clothes and be dressed in such a way that exudes a particular type of elegance and authority. Why? You know that you are coming before an important personality, one of the strongest presidents in the whole world. You can't afford to come there in a careless manner.

## It's a clean place

The Bible tells us in the Scriptures that God is holy and nothing unholy can behold his presence. I want you to look at the Courts of Heaven as a reverential place that only the holy through the blood of Jesus can have access to. If the courts of heaven is a clean place that does not entertain any form of dirt, then it is impossible for any believer who carries any form of impurity in his life to come into that courts and obtained deliverance. This is one important principle that you must understand about praying in the Courts of Heaven. It is important to thoroughly purify your heart from every form of impurity because that is one of the fundamental things that can serve as a hindrance to your prayers there. The Bible tells us that God is too holy to behold any form of unrighteousness and if the prayers in the courts of heaven will matter, then you must be purified.

Another aspect of praying in the courts of heaven is that you cannot go and ask for justice when you have not by yourself shown justice.

# CHAPTER 4

**Note:**

If you have read my **book Prayers for Restoration in The Courts of Heaven**, you might have seen this procedure for entering into the courts of heaven. As a result of the way that this procedure for entering the courts of heaven blessed me, I have decided to bring it here too so that you can be blessed by it. Reading something again for emphases is not a bad thing.

Philippians 3:1

*Finally, my brethren, rejoice in the Lord. To write the same things to you, to me indeed is not grievous, but for you it is safe.*

## Entering the Courts

Before you begin praying in the courts of heaven for anything in your life, the first thing that you need to do is to enter into the courts of heaven. To do that, there are procedures for entrance into the courts of heaven. And unless you follow the procedure for entering into the courts of heaven, any prayer that you pray outside the courts won't be effective as the prayer that was prayed in the courts of heaven.

## The Blood

The Blood of Jesus was not given to us for our redemption alone, it was also given for our purification. The Bible says without the blood of Jesus there can't be any forgiveness of sins. The blood of Jesus is the only ground upon which we can enter into the holies of holy and the courts of heaven to offer our prayers. To this end, before you begin praying in the courts of heaven, ensure that you apply the blood directly to your life. And you do this by pleading the blood of Jesus over your life. In any area of your life that you have sinned against God, you need to ask him for mercies so that the blood can cleanse and wash you from that sin. The Bible says that we should come boldly before the throne of grace that we may find help and grace in the time of need. Do you know that any time that you come before the Lord asking for mercy, you are indeed making demands for the blood of Jesus to come and intervene for you? The blood of Jesus can both wash and cleanse you before you begin your courts of heaven prayer session. Employ the use of the blood of Jesus for your washing and purification. This is the first step towards entering into the courts of heaven. The Bible tells us that the eyes of the Lord are too holy to behold iniquity and if his eyes are too holy to see what is unclean and sinful then that same sin can't come before his courts.

## Invite the Holy Spirit

After making demands for the blood of Jesus to cleanse and purify you from whatever that you have done, the next thing that you need to do is to invite the Holy Spirit. I will be very blunt and frank with you, that without the ministry and the help of the Holy Spirit, it may be impossible to pray effectively in the courts of heaven and see results. The Bible tells us that the Holy Spirit will convict the world of sin and judgment too. Do you remember when you did something or said something you ought not to say and you felt the conviction of the Holy Spirit in your heart rebuking you that what you said was not proper in the circumstance? It may be that what you said wasn't even a sin, but something that the right time to say wasn't ripe or you ought not to have said what you said. And the Holy Spirit instantly performed his ministry of conviction by letting you know straight that you should not talk or say things like that. What the Holy Spirit is doing there is to ensure that you are aligned with God. He knows that there are things that you can say or do which can take you out of alignment with the Lord so he's rebuking you for you to make amends so that your prayers will be very effective any day, any time.

Alignment is the rightness of the heart with the Lord in every area of your life. If you can always keep your heart and your life aligned, the power that your prayers can generate will amaze you.

Friends, before you go into the courts of heaven, ensure that you call on the Holy Spirit to come and then pray that the Holy Spirit, will help you to get aligned with God in all areas of your life. The moment you do and he aligned your heart, your prayers in the courts of heaven will be potent and effective. These are some of the secrets of prayer men and women that pray all the time and see results.

## Faith it Process

One of the essential needs of the life of the believer for life and destiny is called faith. In the book of Hebrews 11:6, the Bible says that if we don't have faith, we can't please God or make him happy. So we need faith to operate in the realm of the spirit and the realm of the earth.  Except the person isn't a believer that is when he will be free to operate by his senses. But as a child of God, faith is necessary for your walk with the Lord and for you to take possession of that which belongs to you.  In the Hall of Faith, the Bible enumerated several men and women of faith who were able to make things happen as a result of their faith in God. The Bible says some of these people shut the mouths of lions, conquered the enemy and destroyed all the barriers that stood in their way.

Hebrews 11:34

*Quenched the violence of fire, escaped the edge of the sword, out of weakness were made strong, waxed valiant in fight, turned to flight the armies of the aliens.*

Someone may think that I entered into the courts of heaven, and I didn't feel anything. The truth is that we as children of God don't walk by feelings but by faith. Sometimes we don't feel like doing certain things but do it because the Holy Spirit wants it done or the word has already commanded us that we should do it. The truth is, if you become a master of your feelings, it may be impossible for you to achieve anything in life. The Bible says he that regards the wind or the rain my not sow and reap.

When it comes to praying in the courts of heaven, your faith is required. You may not see or feel anything but once you have been able to follow the procedure for gaining access into the courts of heaven, then you are there. Don't be a master of your feelings, but a master of your faith.

## Presenter Procedure

If I tell you today that you are to meet the president of the United States for dinner, how would you package yourself? Will you dress in rags to appear before one of the strongest presidents of the world? Will you carelessly come before the president? Are you going to come before the president in the way that you feel like? I am leaving you to answer all of these questions. But I am sure that you won't come before the President of the U.S in that manner. If you won't come before an earthly man like that, how can you come before the Lord, the Kings of Kings, the one that the Bible says, knows the place where the foundation of the earth sank, Jehovah Jireh and Rafa. The manner you come before the courts of heaven and your entering procedure determines whether you can gain access into the courts of heaven. Put yourself together. Put your distractions away from your life. You can't have your phone ringing while you are before the courts of heaven. You put yourself together like a man who is appearing before the highest King. If you don't present yourself well, it is possible not to have access to the courts of heaven where your prayers will be offered.

Friends, the courts of heaven is a great place where prayers are offered. And when you come before the courts of heaven, where God administers the things of the earth and the things that pertain to heaven, then you need to package yourself and present yourself well before the throne of Grace.

# CHAPTER 5

## How to present your prayers in the courts of heaven

Entering into the courts of heaven to pray is one thing, knowing how to present your case before the courts of heaven for an answer is another. While the majority of believers know how to enter into the courts of heaven to present their case before the Lord, the actual presentation of the petition can be flawed thereby rendering the entire process of praying in the courts of heaven ineffective. In reality, every system is governed by principles. That is the reason why you find cultures in different parts of the world and the cultures in those areas of the world governed the conduct of people. A person who had been living in Europe may find something different when it comes to Africa. The same thing goes for the African man who travelled to Europe, some things there may be alien to him. It is for this reason that the believer needs to know that praying in the courts of heaven is governed by certain principles of the Scriptures. We shall be looking at them.

## Presenting your petition by the Scriptures

Your prayers in the Courts of Heaven may be unsuccessful if you don't know how to present your petition before the Lord with scriptural backing. The Bible tells us that let the word of the Lord dwell in our life richly. If a believer must make an impact in any realm of life, one of the first things that he must take hold of is the word of God. The better his understanding of the Scripture and how it relates to his life and circumstances that he is going through, the better he can understand how to present it before the Lord when he goes into the Courts of Heaven. And this is where many a believer has failed. Poor understanding of scripture will lead to the poor outcome of life and even courtroom prayers. I have come to realise that every human being after his adoption into the faith, becomes a lawyer. No lawyer ever goes into the courts of law without first arming himself with the law to present it before the judge. And the sole purpose of that lawyer while presenting his case before the judge is to convince him that he has a better case than the other opponent. And that is the same thing that we do after all as believers, taking back the law of God to him and presenting it before the courts of heaven, justifying by the Scripture why the Lord must act in this way or that way. There is nothing that binds God like his word. The Bible tells us that he exalts his word above his name. That same name that at the mention of the name of Jesus, every knee must bow and every tongue confess that Jesus is Lord. God upholds his word in high regard than his name. So if you're coming before the courts of heaven, and you know the Scriptures to present before the Lord, telling him why he should act and grant your request, you have a higher chance of succeeding than someone who comes before the Lord because he knows how to gain access to the courts of heaven. In every book that I write about the courts of heaven, there are two areas of emphasis that I lay. The first is, how to gain access into the Courts of Heaven and to present your petition. The second is, praying in the Courts of Heaven. I believe that once a believer can comprehend these procedures of the courtroom, he will come out with results. So as a child of God, you need to be armed with the word of God. And when you arrive in the Courts of Heaven the first thing you need to understand is God is bound by his word. A simple prayer in the courts of heaven with Scriptures will make your prayer better. For instance, a believer who is going through financial lack and wants even after obeying all the principles of the covenant that govern the kingdom of God can pray in this manner:

Holy Father, I thank you for the privilege and the opportunity you have given to me to come before the Courts of Heaven and to pray at this time. I am not taking it for granted Lord. I know that by the Scriptures I am supposed to pay my tithes and offerings. You have already promised in your word that if we bring the tithes into your house, you will shower us with blessings. I have obeyed according to your word and since I have done my part, I know that you will not fail in doing yours. Therefore, I am asking you based on the standard of your word as contained in the Holy Scriptures that you break this yoke of financial scarcity off my life and destiny because I have obeyed your word in the name of Jesus.

Another way that the believer can pray before the courts of heaven if he is going through oppression in the dream of the night is this,

Holy Father, I thank you for the wonderful opportunity and privilege that you have given to me to come into your courts at this hour. Let your name be glorified, Lord. You have said in the book of Numbers 26:6 that you will give peace in the land, and I will lie down and nothing shall make me afraid. I have come before the courts of heaven to present these nightmare and horrible dreams I have. This is contrary to the word of the Lord because you have promised to give peace and whenever I lie down, nothing will scare me. Let the power of the Scripture be activated before your courts in my life and let all my dreams be peaceful in the name of Jesus.

Look at the prayers under reference without adequate understanding of the Scriptures can someone pray the prayers? The answer is no. Friends, you will become a better courtroom petitioner if you understand the power of the word of God. If you can present the word of God to him during your prayers in the courts of heaven, he will grant you your heart desires.

## Presenting to the Judge

Luke 18:1-8

*And he spake a parable unto them to this end, that men ought always to pray, and not to faint;*

*2 Saying, There was in a city a judge, which feared not God, neither regarded man:*

*3 And there was a widow in that city; and she came unto him, saying, Avenge me of mine adversary.*

*4 And he would not for a while: but afterward he said within himself, Though I fear not God, nor regard man;*

*5 Yet because this widow troubleth me, I will avenge her,*

*lest by her continual coming she weary me.*

*6 And the Lord said, Hear what the unjust judge saith.*

*7 And shall not God avenge his own elect, which cry day and night unto him, though he bear long with them?*

*8 I tell you that he will avenge them speedily. Nevertheless when the Son of man cometh, shall he find faith on the earth?*

Any time you enter into the courts of heaven, be armed with this understanding that you are coming before a judge that has the power to grant your request. The story of this woman and the unrighteous judge teaches us that anything that you are asking the Lord for he has the power to grant it. Look at how many times the woman in the Bible kept coming before the unjust judge. She was persistent until her request was granted. In the words of the unjust judge, he said if I continue to delay the request of this woman, she will weary me out. If a judge of the earth who is unjust can grant the request of this woman, then God can do more than you can imagine. First, you need to have an idea of the type of judge you are coming before him the Bible tells us that God will do much than we can imagine to his saints who cry before him day and night.

## Standing on justification

Although this is closely related to the word of God, the procedure for praying in the courts of heaven when you are standing on justification is a little bit different. Here, you are asking the Lord to justify by the standard of his word whether something should be permitted or not. You are saying Lord, based on the standard of your word should this be permitted? And if the answer to the prayers I have put before the courts of heaven is no, then this should not be permitted to stand either in my life or the lives of my loved ones.

But I want you to understand that every justification is not based on facts alone. By facts, I mean the situation that you are currently going through or what you have come before the courts of heaven to present before the Lord. Your justification should be based on Scriptures whether it is permissible according to the word of God or not. If it is permissible according to the word of the Lord, then let it stand. But if it is not permissible according to God's word, let that thing fall apart. Again, the right understanding of the Scripture to use for justification is very important. If you are praying in the courts of heaven against witchcraft for instance, what Scripture should govern your prayers? Of course, there is a popular Scripture that we often quote, suffer the witch not to live. Another Scripture goes, whatever is permitted on the earth, is permitted in heaven. And whatever it is refused on the earth, it is also refused in the heavens. A believer who is standing upon these two Scriptures justifying why witchcraft oppression should not continue in his life will simply pray like this,

Holy Father, I have come before your courts at this time to present this case of witchcraft oppression in my life. I have seen from the Scriptures that the witch is not permitted to live and the sentence for every witchcraft Practitioner is death if that person refuses to repent. By the standard of your word, I pray at this moment whether it is permissible for this witchcraft oppression to continue in my life in the name of Jesus.

This is how to pray by justification when you are before the courts of heaven. You are simply telling the Lord to act based on the standard of his word whether the thing should stand or not. And we have already established that God exalts his word above his name. The Bible further tells us that, the word of the Lord is settled in the heavens. That is the power of praying in the courts of heaven by justification.

## Intercessory Justification

Intercessory justification becomes very useful for someone who is praying in the Courts of Heaven for another person. Most of the times, you hear believers say can you pray for me or join me in faith and pray over this particular issue. Well if you are praying other types of prayers that do not involve the courts of heaven, you can go ahead and pray it. But if you are coming before the Courts of Heaven to pray for that person, how do you do it? There is a way to pray in the courts of heaven for another person. And that is where intercessory justification becomes very important. There is something important the Bible says in the Scriptures, that I sought for a man who will stand in the gap that I should not destroy the land but I found none.

Ezekiel 22:30

> *And I sought for a man among them, that should make up the hedge, and stand in the gap before me for the land, that I*

*should not destroy it: but I found none.*

So because of one man, land can be spared. If you are praying for your family, intercessory justification is the way to go. By this manner of prayers in the Courts of Heaven, you are telling God simply that based on the standard of your word that this is not permitted to happen to the person I'm praying for. Or you are asking God to justify whether this is okay or not. Again, understanding the Scripture to use for intercessory justification is a very important factor here. If you are praying for a loved one, the Bible has already given us a direction on what to do. Once you understand these principles of coming before the courtroom of heaven to pray for prayers, you are going to become an effective courtroom prayer warrior. As I have said earlier, it is not all about going into the courts of heaven to pray, how you pray is also important. And this is what this book is teaching you how to pray in the Courts of heaven effectively whether as a beginner or a courtroom prayer warrior. Although the prayer that Abraham prayed for his cousin Lot did not take place in the courts of heaven, it teaches us something about intercessory justification. Abraham started by pleading with God to consider the fact that it is impossible based on the standard of the word of God to destroy both the righteous and the wicked together. In the words of Abraham, let it be far from you to destroy both the righteous and the wicked. But what was Abraham trying to do? He was using intercessory justification. Abraham was telling God that Lord, if you feel that it is justifiable to consume the land of Sodom and Gomorrah with my cousin Lot who has been living righteously, then you can go ahead and do it.

2 Peter 2:7-8

> *And delivered just Lot, vexed*
> *with the filthy conversation of*
> *the wicked:*

> *8 (For that righteous man dwelling among them, in seeing and hearing, vexed his righteous soul from day to day with their unlawful deeds;)*

If it is not, then don't do it. If you look at that Scripture very well, Abraham did not conclude with God. The Bible says he left talking with the Lord. After he had adequately presented his matter before the throne of grace, he left it for God to decide whether it is proper according to the standard of the word of the Lord to act either in this manner or that way. And did the Lord listen to the intercessory justification of Abraham? Of course, he did. In subsequent chapters of the Bible, we will see that God deployed angels to come and save Lot, his cousin.

Friends, if you want to become a better intercessor in the courts of heaven concerning the burden of others or that of your loved ones, then you must understand the basis of intercessory justification and how to present it before the courts of heaven. This is a very important principle if you will be successful in courtroom prayers for others.

# CHAPTER 5

## Prayers in the Courts

Now, it is time to pray in the courts of heaven and this way of praying is going to be different from all that you have ever prayed in our courts of heaven series.

## Reflection

Isaiah 65:24

> *And it shall come to pass, that before they call, I will answer; and while they are yet speaking, I will hear.*

Isaiah 41:21

> *Produce your cause, saith the Lord; bring forth your strong reasons, saith the King of Jacob.*

Holy Father, I thank you for the opportunity and privilege that you have given to me to come before the courts of heaven at this moment to you be all the glory and the honour in the mighty name of Jesus.

Heavenly Father, I stand before the courts of heaven knowing that the scripture and the word of the Lord cannot be broken. I pray for this so... (mention the name of the person you are praying for)  that you will cause a manifestation of the word of the Lord to be performed in the life of this person knowing that by the standard of your word that he is not supposed to be going through what he has been going through in the name of Jesus.

Gracious Father, I come before you at this hour to pray for (state the person's name) member of my family because I have seen from your word that what you are seeking for is just a man that will stand in the gap so that the entire land can be spared. I make demands for this member of my family that the devil has been attacking from left, right and every direction that you will cause all the attacks of the devil to cease and let your peace flow into his life in the name of Jesus.

Holy Father, I come before the courts of heaven at this time and pray for (mention the name of the person) who has been harassed and dominated by the spirit of infirmity. I stand before the courts of heaven based on the standard of your word in the Bible that you have died so that infirmity can no longer have its way in our lives. I pray today that the grip of the spirit of infirmity is broken over the life of this person in the name of Jesus.

Holy Father, I come before the courts of heaven to pray at this hour that you will cause a quick performance of your word in the life of (state the name of the person); I know this person, he has been observing all financial covenant practices that should bring in financial abundance including tithing. Now, Lord, I pray that you will judge according to the standard of your word whether it is good for... (Mention the name of the person) who applied the word of the Lord in his life to continue to suffer lack and financial shortage in his life in the name of Jesus.

Holy Father, I make demands in the courts of heaven at this hour that a speedy divine intervention will come through for (state the person's name) who has been seeking your face for the upliftment in his business today in the name of Jesus.

Gracious Father, I come before you to pray for my daughter/son that a divine rescue will occur speedily in their lives to keep them from making mistakes that will damage their lives and destiny in the name of Jesus.

Thank you, Lord, for hearing and answering me in the courts of heaven in the name of Jesus.

**Prayers by Decrees**

**Reflection**

*Job 22:28*

> *Thou shalt also decree a thing, and it shall be established unto thee: and the light shall shine upon thy ways.*

Proverbs 8:29

> *When he gave to the sea his decree, that the waters should not pass his commandment: when he appointed the foundations of the earth:*

**Prayers**

Holy Father, I thank you for the privilege that you have given to me to come before the courts of heaven to pray by decrees in the name of Jesus.

Glorious Father, I decree before the courts of heaven that the days of oppression (financial oppression, mind oppression, oppression in dreams, oppression in my business, etc.) be over today in the name of Jesus.

Glorious Father, I decree today in the courts of heaven that you will cause a flow of fresh grace to be poured upon my life and destiny in the name of Jesus.

Righteous Father, I pray today that every yoke that the enemy has placed upon my life, I decree in the courts of heaven that it is broken in the name of Jesus.

Holy Father, I decree today before the throne of grace in the courts of heaven that every spirit of disfavour that the devil has placed around my life be consumed by fire in the name of Jesus.

Holy Father, I decree and declare that every limitation that the enemy has placed on my life and destiny is destroyed in the courts of heaven in the name of Jesus.

Glorious Father, every wrong identity that the enemy has placed on my life so that what should not be happening to me is now the norm in my life, by the authority in the name of Jesus the wrong identity is broken in the name of Jesus.

Holy Father, I stand before the courts of heaven today, and I decree that every trap that the enemy has set in my path so that I would continue to be a victim of repeated negative cycles, I decree and declare that they are destroyed in the name of Jesus.

Righteous Father, I come before your throne this day and I decree that every generational curse that has been moving from one family to another in my bloodline, I decree today that it is broken in the name of Jesus.

Heavenly Father, I decree today before the courts of heaven that divine speed will come into my life that I can achieve all that I need to achieve for my life and destiny in the name of Jesus.

Holy Father, I decree today that anything that has been speaking into my life in the realm of the spirit, those negative proclamations are destroyed in the courts of heaven in the name of Jesus

Thank You, Lord, for hearing and answering my prayers in the courts of heaven to you be all the glory in the name of Jesus.

## Praying By Restraining Order

You can pray by restraining order in the courts of heaven to forbid or command the occurrence of a thing. And we shall be praying in the courts of heaven now.

## Reflection

Matthew 16:19

> *And I will give unto thee the keys of the kingdom of heaven: and whatsoever thou shalt bind on earth shall be bound in heaven: and whatsoever thou shalt loose on earth shall be loosed in heaven.*

Luke 10:19

> *Behold, I give unto you power to tread on serpents and scorpions, and over all the power of the enemy: and nothing shall by any means hurt you.*

**Prayers**

Holy Father, I stand today in the courts of heaven and restrain every arrow of death that the enemy has fired into my life, the lives of my family and loved ones in the name of Jesus.

Heavenly Father, I pray in the courts of heaven and I restrain every spirit of premature death that has been operating in the life of my family and destiny in the name of Jesus.

Glorious Father, I stand before the courts of heaven at this hour and I restrain every arrow of financial attacks fired by the enemy into my life, that arrow is restrained from gaining expression in my life and destiny in the name of Jesus.

Holy Father, I stand today before the courts of heaven and I restrain every arrow of confusion that the enemy has fired into my life and destiny in the name of Jesus.

Holy Father, I stand before the courts of heaven and I pray to restrain every witchcraft coven from operating against my life today in the name of Jesus.

Glorious Father, I stand today before the courts of heaven and restrain every satanic door that wants to open against my life and destiny in the name of Jesus.

Thank you, Lord, for hearing and answering my prayers in the name of Jesus.

## Prayers by Binding Orders

The Bible says that whatever that we bound on earth, it is bound in heaven and whatever we lose on earth, is also lose in heaven. By this scripture, we can bind things in heaven and it will be bound and that is what we are going to be doing in the courts of heaven right now.

## Reflection

Mark 3:27

> *No man can enter into a strong man's house, and spoil his goods, except he will first bind the strong man; and then he will spoil his house.*

Proverbs 6:5

> *Deliver thyself as a roe from*
> *the hand of the hunter, and as*
> *a bird from the hand of the*
> *fowler.*

Holy Father, I stand today before the courts of heaven and bind all the works of darkness that have been standing against my life in the name of Jesus.

Holy Father, every satanic network that the devil has been using to work against my life and destiny, today they are bound in the name of Jesus.

Gracious Father, I pray today before the courts of heaven, every spirit that has been sent to frustrate my life and destiny, they are bound in the name of Jesus.

Holy Father, I bind every spirit that has been sent to monitor my life and destiny so that they will release information back to the kingdom of darkness in the name of Jesus.

Glorious Father, I bind every spirit of infirmity out of my life now in the name of Jesus.

Holy Father, I bind every spirit of dryness out of my life and destiny in the name of Jesus.

Holy Father, I stand before the courts of heaven and bind every spirit of insanity out of my family lineage in the name of Jesus.

Holy Father, I stand before the courts of heaven and bind every wall of resistance standing against my life and destiny in the name of Jesus.

Heavenly Father, every strong man (human or demonic) standing watch and preventing us from accessing all that belongs to us, today I stand in the courts of heaven and bind that strong man in the name of Jesus.

Thank you, for I know that everything that has been bound in the courts of heaven is also bound on the earth in the name of Jesus.

## Important Decision

If you are reading this book and you are not saved, pray this prayer after me:

Lord Jesus, I come before you today. I give you my heart. I give you my all. Come into my life. Become my Lord and saviour. Deliver me from the power of sin. Help me to live for you forever, in Jesus name.

## Prayer

Let us know about your prayer needs as our team add you to our prayer list and intercede fervently on your behalf.

Also, check our blog for Holy Ghost inspired content.

www.thetentofglory.com

I would love to hear from you how our ministry and our books have blessed you. Write to us at

pius@thetentofglory.com

## Our Books

1.  Obtaining Restoration in the Courts of Heaven: Courtroom Prayers for All Round Restoration

2.  Witchcraft Summons: Prayers for Overpowering witchcraft Summons & Refusing to Answer their Call

3.  Monitoring Spirits: Prayers for Destroying Monitoring Spirits and Receiving Deliverance

4.  Evil Gatekeepers: Prayers to Break Free, Enter and Possess what's Yours

5.  Overthrowing Evil Altars Secrets Revealed: Prayers for Dismantling Evil Altars

6.  Praying the Blood of Jesus the Right Way: Pleading the Blood of Jesus for Turnaround

7.  Prayers that Destroy Water Spirits: Freedom from marine Kingdom and Marine Spirits

79

Pius Joseph

81

83

84